FROM BROKE TO AN ABUNDANCE MINDSET

If You Don't Try You Will Never Change

Zeelah S. Davis

Published by:

ISBN: 978-1-958404-56-0 (paperback)

Scripture quotations marked "KJV" are taken from the Holy Bible,
King James Version (Public Domain).

All Scripture quotations are taken from THE MESSAGE, copyright
© 1993, 2002, 2018 by Eugene H. Peterson. Used by permission of
NavPress. All rights reserved. Represented by Tyndale House
Publishers, Inc.

Scripture quotations marked (NIV) are taken from the Holy Bible,
New International Version®, NIV®. Copyright © 1973, 1978, 1984
by Biblica, Inc.™ Used by permission of Zondervan. All rights
reserved worldwide.

Scripture quotations taken from the Amplified® Bible (AMP).
Copyright © 2015 by The Lockman Foundation. Used by
permission. www.Lockman.org.

TABLE OF CONTENTS

PREFACE

To my wife on our 25th wedding anniversary and renewal of vows:

I choose you again

I choose you again from the blossoms in the field
Your beauty and your radiance you continue to reveal.

Perfectly aged with time
Like fine wine
Specially picked for a day like today, oh so divine.

A virtuous woman I have found, placed on a hill so bright
Not under a bushel but in the open
For your stunning bright light.

I choose you, again
Like Priscilla and Aquila
And their true one-flesh oneness
Continue steadfastly on your journey
To be an example to others of true righteousness.

I choose you, again

I have tried what seems to be an experiment of marriage and one flesh
And I affirm to you that I am stuck
It's not an experiment but truly a success.

I choose you, again

Twenty-five years have flown by so miraculously fast
And the ups and downs, we have left in the past.

I affirm that by God we can now leap over a wall
And come out on the other side standing tall.

I choose you, again.

INTRODUCTION

I remember being in a full hour-and-a-half presentation listening to three so-called financial experts. They meandered through their deck of slides explaining how they can make you rich with the many products they offer at their prestigious financial management company. No doubt they had gone over these slides countless times, and with repetition and time, their art of delivery had become excellent. When question and answer time came, they were eager to answer the questions from the audience. No doubt, there was not a question that could reach them that they had not answered many times before and, just like they did on previous occasions, they were going to be able to hit a home run with a masterful stroke of an answer. This time they were wrong.

A middle-aged gentleman raised his hand, and when it was time for him to ask his question, he said. "Sir, can I walk with you to your car when you are heading out? I want to see what you drive." The room went silent. The presenters looked at each other in bewilderment. They had never received a request like that before. To break the air, the youngest of the presenters, A young lady in her twenties, asked why he wanted to see what her co-worker drove. The gentlemen then proceeded to answer: "If you can offer us the level of financial wealth that you are presenting, then certainly you would have used this knowledge to your own benefit." The room again became silent. This time, the lead presenter chuckled and asked, "Can we get a serious question?" and quickly moved to answer the other questions presented to them.

When the presenters were leaving, the middle-aged gentleman did tag along with them as they moved to the parking lot. They beckoned to the security guard to open the gate and they were gone. Based on what the gentlemen saw, he concluded that he could not take this financial company seriously, and he did not move on to access any of the services they had presented.

One reality of life is that people lie a lot, and they tend to appeal to our emotions to sway us to make decisions that are in their favor. These actions may not be beneficial to you in most instances. It pays when you are financially educated so you can make decisions that are in the best interest of achieving your financial goals.

I do not claim to be a financial expert in any way, shape, or form. All the material presented in this book is easy to follow and straight to the facts. They are intended to change your mindset and cause you to build a new relationship with money and wealth.

It is time to go against the grain and decide what kind of life you want to live, then pursue it unapologetically.

CHAPTER 1

WE ALL NEED A LOT OF MONEY

Many people spend their entire life chasing money, sacrificing their time, health, and relationships in the process. We always seem to want more, and we tie this to happiness in a one-to-one direct correlation where the more we have, the happier we get.

While money is undoubtedly important, it should not be the sole focus of one's life. Having financial stability is necessary, but it should not come at the cost of our well-being and relationships. We should prioritize our health and happiness.

Instead of solely focusing on accumulating wealth, we should strive for a balanced life where we prioritize our mental and emotional health, relationships with loved ones, and passions and hobbies. Finding a purpose and meaning in life that goes beyond just making money is crucial.

At the end of the day, life is not just about the amount of money we have but the experiences we have had, the relationships we have built, and the impact we have had in our surroundings.

But if it's only money these leaders are after, they'll self-destruct in no time. Lust for money brings trouble and nothing but trouble. Going down that path, some lose their footing in the faith completely and live to regret it bitterly ever after. (1 Timothy 6:10 – MSG).

CHAPTER 2

HOW MUCH MONEY DO YOU NEED TO MAKE TO GUARANTEE HAPPINESS

I would be happy to tell you that money does not guarantee happiness, but I cannot. A study on happiness, income satiation, and turning points around the world has shown that the opposite is true, and the amount of money you have can determine your happiness. While the study proved that money makes you happier, it showed that this is true only up to a point. The study of 1.7 million people showed that life satisfaction peaked at around US$95,000 per year, and emotional well-being was also satisfied at US$60,000 to $75,000.

A separate study from Princeton University conducted by economist, Angus Deaton, and psychologist, Daniel Kahneman, showed that the lower a person's annual income falls below US$75,000, the unhappier the individual will feel. The surprising result, however, is that as the income amount increases above US$75,000, the same results occur with people not feeling happy anymore.

This is a startling result as one would have expected a more direct correlation between money and happiness with you experiencing more happiness as your financial wealth increases in life. The truth is, money makes you happy, but it is the specific amount of US$75,000 that makes you happy. So, if you are lucky enough to have US$75,000 in your bank account, you will be one of those who will reap happiness. With that level of subjectivity, I would conclude that generally, money does not make you happy. So, if money does not make you happy, then what does it do? I think it creates the opportunity to find contentment and supply you with everything you need to exist.

For the love of money is the root of all evil: which while some coveted after, they have erred from the faith, and pierced themselves through with many sorrows. (1 Timothy 6:10 – KJV).

One of the things that often happens is, when a financial increase comes, we try to acquire more and more until we are back to the same position we were in before, with more bills and less money to spend. It is best to stay at the same level before and after the increase as you will have better spending power.

Study Of Lottery Winners

Over the past couple of years, several news organizations have attributed a statistic to the National Endowment for Financial Education (NEFE) that states that 70% of lottery winners end up bankrupt in just a few years after receiving a large financial windfall.

There have been numerous stories of how people's lives changed for the WORSE by winning millions. Some reports advise that before you think that winning the lottery would solve all your problems, think again.

Some financial advisors recommend that you invest your time in learning a new skill to build up your CV and knowledge. With this, you can get a better-paying job or be able to put that skill to work in your personal business endeavors.

Generational Wealth

Smart investments and money management skills are not always passed down with wealth. A staggering 70% of wealthy families lose their wealth by the next generation, with 90% losing it the generation after that. Sustaining substantial wealth takes financial savvy–something not all rich parents are passing along to their heirs.[1]

Studies on the effect of adversity on people have concluded that hardships can help people become more successful because having to face adversity can teach us valuable lessons that we would not have learned otherwise. For example, when we face challenges or obstacles, we might

---

[1] 5 Huge Lies About Generational Wealth, Sam DiSalvo, October 1, 2021

learn to become more resilient, determined, and creative in finding solutions.

Adversity can also help us to develop important life skills, such as problem-solving, critical thinking, and decision-making. These skills are highly valued and can be useful in personal life. Many successful people have even credited their difficult experiences as being major contributors to their achievements and accomplishments.

However, it is important to keep in mind that not everyone who faces hardships will necessarily become more successful as a result. The way people respond to adversity can vary greatly. Additionally, some people might be more prone to the negative effects of adversity, such as trauma and stress.

People need to educate themselves about money management to make informed decisions and achieve financial independence. This includes understanding how to create and stick to a budget, managing debt, saving for the future, investing wisely, and protecting assets through insurance. It is important to regularly review and adjust financial plans. As circumstances change, seek advice from professionals as needed. By taking the time to educate themselves, individuals can gain the confidence and knowledge needed to make sound financial decisions and achieve their financial goals. Likewise, it is also important for parents and guardians to make it a priority, along with ensuring that their children have enough money to offer them a sound financial future, to ensure they are equipped with the skills of money management and, more importantly, how to retain the wealth they will receive.

How much money do you need to make you happy?

_____

_____

_____

_____

_____

_____

_____

_____

_____

_____

_____

_____

_____

_____

_____

_____

_____

_____

_____

CHAPTER 3

WHY WE DON'T LEARN ABOUT MONEY IN SCHOOL

Nobody wants to hear this, but schools teach you to be poor, not to be rich.

One would think that a school would be the source of important life-skills, including teaching sound financial management that would prepare you for the future. However, this does not seem to be the case. They don't teach you how to make money work for you, but they teach you how to work for money. They don't teach you how to create and generate wealth. They teach you how to be a good employee but not how to be creative in starting your own business and being an employer.

History shows that schools were created in England during the industrialization period to satisfy the present and future needs of workers to work in the factories.

Factory owners required docile, agreeable workers who would show up on time and do what their managers told them. Sitting in a classroom all day with a teacher was good training for that. Early industrialists were instrumental in creating and promoting universal education. The modern education system was designed to teach future factory workers to be "punctual, docile, and sober."[2]

John Davison Rockefeller was an American business magnate. He has been widely considered the wealthiest American of all time and the richest person in history. This is what he had to say, "I don't want a nation of thinkers. I want a nation of workers."

Rockefeller not only made his thoughts vocal, but he also backed this up with an investment of 128 million dollars to the General Education Board that he founded in 1902.

Imagine the difference it would make if we were all taught the following skills very early in our teen years:

1. Money management
2. Interpersonal skills
3. Innovation
4. Investing
5. Budgeting
6. Saving

The bottom line is, if we are taught financial literacy, the market will lose customers and it would lose workers. It is

---

[2] Allison Schrager, June 29, 2018

said that it is profitable to keep people poor and financially illiterate because if you understand money, then you can use it to your advantage. Also, the less educated you are, the easier you are to control.

I am in no way saying that school is not important. My schooling took me all the way up to university, and both of my children are enrolled in high school and also looking toward a university education. It is time, however, to change the way you think. Begin to question what you have been taught, unlearn the system of factory workers, and increase your learning of the skills that lead to financial literacy and abundance and away from poverty.

School is not the only place you get an education, and the saying of the University of Life depicts this very well. You must move beyond the school system, learn from people who are successful in what they do, and apply to your life some of what they did. Learn from successful entrepreneurs. Learn from successful investment advisors.

The book of Proverbs outlines how one's life is ruined because they do not heed the voice of wisdom of persons who have walked the path before us that have experienced and lived success.

...Why should you allow strangers to take advantage of you? Why be exploited by those who care nothing for you? You don't want to end your life full of regrets, nothing but sin and bones, Saying, "Oh,

why didn't I do what they told me? Why did I reject a disciplined life? Why didn't I listen to my mentors, or take my teachers seriously? My life is ruined! I haven't one blessed thing to show for my life!" (Proverbs 5:7-14 – MSG).

CHAPTER 4

WHY IS MONEY IMPORTANT?

The reality of our present life is that more money brings more respect from others, and those who have more money have more power. This is in stark contrast to the YouTube channel for Trip2Wealth, which offers financial guidance. In their focus on the rules of money, they strongly advise in their first rule of money to not let anyone know you have money, and not to draw attention to yourself.

"Take care! Protect yourself against the least bit of greed. Life is not defined by what you have, even when you have a lot." (Luke 12:15b – MSG).

According to Robert Kiyosaki of the "Rich Dad Poor Dad" fame, money is not the most important thing in life, but it does affect everything that is important.

Regarding the worldview of money bringing respect and power, I believe this is brought on by our education system, which results in people developing an employee mindset versus an employer mindset, as I outlined in Chapter 3.

With an employer-mindset, people take ownership. As an employer, you take ownership of your decisions and the outcomes of your business and don't wait for someone else to make decisions for you.

An employer thinks strategically. They think about where they want their business to be in the future and how they can get there. They create a plan and focus on achieving goals.

An employer hires the right people. They recognize that their staff is the backbone of their business. They hire people who share their vision, are passionate about the business, and have the skills and experience needed to help the business succeed.

An employer manages their finances proactively. They keep track of their expenses, create a budget, and make sure their cash flow is healthy.

An employer focuses on growth. They never stop growing. They continuously look for ways to improve their business and stay ahead of the competition.

An employer is resilient. They know that running a business is not easy, and there will be challenges along the way. They are resilient and willing to adapt to change.

An employer takes calculated risks. They are aware that they need to take calculated risks to grow their business. They are not afraid to try new things and make sure they have a plan in place.

An employer thinks long-term. They don't make decisions based on short-term gains. They focus on building a sustainable business that will thrive for years to come.

You may have realized above that the employer is someone who has confidence in themselves, is self-disciplined, and they never shy away from leading. These are the skills that should be the focus of our educational system to prepare future leaders.

An employer's mindset does not mean everyone will end up being an employer or that you cannot work in someone else's business as an employee. What it means, however, is that you have the skills and experience required to deliver success to yourself and your employer's business.

Don't be the person who uses money as a status thing!

One day as I was observing how wisdom fares on this earth, I saw something that made me sit up and take notice. There was a small town with only a few people in it. A strong king came and mounted an attack, building trenches and attack posts around it. There was a poor but wise man in that town whose wisdom saved the town, but he was promptly forgotten. (He was only a poor man, after all.) All the same, I still say that wisdom is better than muscle, even though the wise poor man was treated

with contempt and soon forgotten. (Ecclesiastes 9:13-16
– MSG).

Why is money important to you?

_____

_____

_____

_____

_____

_____

_____

_____

_____

_____

_____

_____

_____

_____

_____

_____

_____

_____

_____

_____

_____

CHAPTER 5

SHORTAGE OF SKILLS/TRADE WORKERS

In 2021, 88% of contractors reported significant difficulty finding qualified workers versed in trades like plumbing and carpentry. According to the US Chamber of Commerce data, 73% of contractors cited the worker shortage as their greatest concern in 2022.

This has always been a problem, as over the years there has been a steady migration of workers from construction sites into the boardroom and blue-collar workers to white-collar workers as the new entrants into the job market joined the prestigious lifestyle depicted by millennials in popular sitcoms. The pandemic made the matter worst and caused a major disruption in America's labor force. This is often referred to as The Great Resignation.[3]

---

[3] Stephanie Ferguson, Director in the article titled Global Employment Policy & Special Initiatives, U.S. Chamber of Commerce, Published March 23, 2023.

In 2022, more than 50 million workers quit their jobs, many of whom were in search of an improved work-life balance and flexibility, increased compensation, and a strong company culture.

The shortage of skilled workers provides an opportunity for people looking to enter or pivot their careers. One of the main benefits of a shortage of skilled workers is that it can increase demand for individuals with certain skills or expertise, leading to higher wages and better job security. This can be especially beneficial for people who are looking to enter a new career or who have taken the time to develop their skills in a particular field.

Additionally, employers may be more willing to offer training programs or other opportunities for professional development to attract and retain skilled workers. This can be an excellent opportunity for individuals looking to learn new skills or expand their knowledge base.

Overall, while shortages of skilled workers can create challenges for employers, they can also provide opportunities for individuals looking to enter new careers or develop their skills.

As we look at moving to an abundance mindset, I have chosen to include this information on the shortage of skilled and trade workers so people can see that the opportunities that exist for them extend way beyond the boardroom. The reality of the jobs available in these fields is that they are in demand and often offer greater financial rewards than office jobs.

Recently I was watching a YouTube channel that focuses on the business of being a handyman, and they indicated that they can make up to two hundred dollars (US$200) per hour for simple household repairs.

Don't limit yourself to only office jobs but expand your opportunities into skill and trade work.

CHAPTER 6

APPRENTICESHIP

Ll schools should have apprenticeship built into their curriculum.

Apprenticeship can provide students with practical, real-world experiences that can help them develop important workplace skills and gain valuable insight into potential career paths. By incorporating apprenticeship into school curriculums, students will have the opportunity to gain valuable workplace experience while still pursuing their education.

Apprenticeship may help better align education with workforce needs, creating a bridge between academic learning and job readiness. When students participate in apprenticeship opportunities, they can better understand the requirements and expectations of different fields, which can lead to more informed career choices.

Apprenticeship may provide opportunities for students to earn money while expanding their skillset. This can be particularly important for students from low-income backgrounds who may face financial barriers to pursuing higher education or training.

There are some professors and teachers who believe that apprenticeship should be strongly marketed as an alternative to college.

Learn A Skill/Trade

There are benefits to working with your hands. It is true that working with your hands is a skill you can never lose. Once you learn a skill that requires physical dexterity, such as woodworking or sewing, you will likely retain that skill throughout your life. Even if you don't practice the skill for an extended period of time, you will usually be able to pick it back up relatively quickly because the muscle memory and neural connections developed in the brain remain intact even if you haven't used the skill in a while. In addition, many people find that working with their hands can be therapeutic and enjoyable, making it a skill they are likely to continue using and practicing for many years to come.

It is said that the skills you do with your hands will never be redundant as they will always be needed resulting in them being a sure source of employment and income. When the country experiences a recession and corporate white-collar employers have to make a vast number of staff redundant, these are skills that we can never do without.

How long can one survive without water if they have a leaking pipe that cuts the water supply to their home? You will always need a plumber. Even if you decide to do the work yourself, you are the plumber.

How long can you survive the intense cold of the winter if there is a leak in your gas line starving your furnace of much needed supply to radiate warmth in your home? Not to mention the safety hazard posed to you and your family by that gas leak. You will always need someone to repair the gas line.

How long can you endure a leaking roof causing flooding inside your home, resulting in the possibility of mold build-up that can be disastrous to your health? You will always need a roofer.

Here are some benefits that people could gain by pursuing a trade:

1. Job security: As trades are key pillars of infrastructure, there is always a demand for skilled workers in various fields. This means that trade professionals typically enjoy job security, even during tough economic times.

2. Hands-on experience: Trade education is heavily focused on experiential learning, providing students with hands-on training that equips them with skills they can apply instantly in the workplace.

3. Higher income: Trained tradespeople typically earn high wages, especially if they have obtained licensure or certification; these credentials often result in higher pay.

4. Independence: Many trades offer the opportunity for self-employment, which enables professionals to run their own businesses, make their own decisions, and set their own schedules.

5. Rapid career growth: There are plenty of opportunities for advancement in trade careers, from apprentices to journeymen to master-level positions, giving workers a clear path to career progression.

6. Active work: Trade jobs are generally quite physical, requiring workers to be on their feet and engaged throughout their workday. This can be beneficial for people who enjoy active and practical work, rather than a desk-bound job.

Learn a skill today!

Find an apprenticeship opportunity for your children to learn a skill today.

What skill/trade do you want to learn?

_____

_____

_____

_____

_____

_____

_____

_____

_____

_____

_____

_____

_____

_____

_____

_____

_____

_____

_____

CHAPTER 7

BUILDING A RELATIONSHIP WITH MONEY

Some people believe that having money means that as soon as they get it, they should spend it. Individuals need to have a healthy relationship with money and not fall into the trap of spending all their income without considering their financial goals.

Having money means you have been provided with the ability to make choices that can positively impact your financial situation, such as investing in a business venture. Spending money without a plan can lead to financial stress, debt, and missed opportunities.

It is important to remember that there is nothing wrong with spending money on things that bring joy and value, as long as it aligns with your financial goals and budget. However, it is also vital to develop good money habits to ensure long-term financial stability.

While spending is one way to use money, it is not the only way. Money can be saved, invested, donated, or used to pay off debts, among other things. Also, money does not necessarily have to be spent to have value. So, it is important to remember that money does not only equal spending, but it also has other valuable purposes.

Here are some ways that you can establish a healthy relationship with money:

1. Understand your values and priorities. Knowing what is important to you will help you make smart decisions when it comes to what should be spent and what needs to be saved.

2. Tracking your income and expenses by creating a budget. This can help you manage your money better and avoid overspending.

3. Set financial goals. Whether it is paying off debt, saving for an emergency fund, or investing in your future, having specific financial goals can help you stay focused and motivated.

4. Educate yourself. Learn about personal finance and investment strategies so you can make informed decisions and maximize your financial potential.

5. Be mindful of your spending habits. Practice self-awareness and mindfulness when it comes to your

spending habits. Ask yourself before making a purchase, do I really need this? Will this add value to my life?

6. Give back. Give back to society or your community by contributing to social causes or charitable organizations. It will give you a sense of purpose and satisfaction.

Remember, money is a tool, not a measure of your worth. Don't let your financial situation define your self-worth. Be kind to yourself and focus on your progress and achievements.

CHAPTER 8

UNDERSTANDING YOUR MONEY

Some people believe that money makes you evil and, quite often, this is borne out of a lack of knowledge based on their source of information.

I often share with others a video of an interview with a very popular music artist. During the interview, when the matter of money came up, the artist said with confidence that "Money is the root of all evil." No doubt he was trying to reflect a scripture from the Bible. However, the correct wording of the scripture, according to 1 Timothy 6:10, states **"For the love of money is the root of all evil:" (KJV).** Take note of the words "for the love of" that were omitted from the artist's statement. These words totally change the meaning of the sentence, moving the emphasis from money as evil to the love of money being evil. I can only assume that the person had a senior moment, and this was a common mistake. However, imagine the many followers this person has who take whatever they say as gospel now accepting the evil of money and that it is evil to make money.

Always validate your source of information!

Another area of understanding your money is knowing where your money comes from, where it is going, and where you want it to go. This will help you make more informed decisions and prevent any surprises.

Before money existed, people had to do what was termed bartering. For example, if a person was a farmer and needed his car fixed, he could trade some of the food from his farm as payment to the mechanic for repairing his vehicle. This facilitated exchange as a measure of value.

With the creation of money, there was now a common index spanning across all societies, communities, careers, and disciplines that persons could now trade. The farmer no longer had to wait to find a mechanic that needed his farm produce; he would now have his vehicle repaired by any mechanic and pay them cash.

Money allows people to trade goods and services indirectly. It helps communicate the price of goods and provides individuals with a way to store their wealth.[4]

With the creation of money came banks whose intent was to offer secure storage for the money for wealthy people.

---

[4] The History of Money By ANDREW BEATTIE Updated September 17, 2022

Empires also needed a financial system to facilitate trade, distribute wealth, and collect taxes.

Having money was not an impediment to you doing trade as banks were more than willing to lend you money. With this came bankers, and bankers are not your financial advisors. Whereas your financial advisor will guide you on how to create wealth with the money you have, bankers are in the business of making their commission as a percentage of the amount of money they can get you to borrow from their banks. The more money you borrow, the more commission they make. I am sure you can imagine the amount of greed and selfishness that can develop in a situation like this, and the more gullible and less informed you are, the greater will be the financial hole that you find yourself in.

Bankers are not your financial advisors!

CHAPTER 9

INVESTING MEANS I WILL LOSE MY MONEY

"Get a good job, work hard, put your money in a bank, and just leave it."

Many of us can remember this as the first and most important financial advice given to us by our parents when we got our first job. This was a single strategy known by our parents as this was no doubt handed down to them by their parents who received the same advice from their parents. Their understanding was putting your money in the bank was the safest way to get rich, and anything else would lead to you losing money by being ripped off by some unscrupulous individual.

Our parents did not understand the principle of investing and were quick to say it was a no-no. Saving was a strategy many of us tried, and we soon came to realize that the measly percentage interest banks gave us on our savings did not amount to anything. The stark difference between what they gave you and what they required you to give them when you took out a loan with them for your first car was startling. There must be a better way as the safe way your parents spoke about was not working.

Investing

Investing is putting money into financial schemes, shares, property, or a commercial venture with the expectation of achieving a profit.

Investing is an effective way to put your money to work and build wealth by growing it while you are sleeping. One good thing about investing is that it does not require your active participation.

Investing always involves a certain degree of risk, and there is always the possibility of losing money. However, it is important to remember that investing is also a way to potentially grow your money over the long term.

It is important that when you think of investing, you understand that investing is indeed a long-term strategy. You should not expect that you will invest today and become a millionaire overnight. Just like a farmer when he plants his crops, a certain amount of time must pass before he can reap the crop. This time is dependent on the type of crop planted. In the case of vegetables, most take 6-8 months before the harvest. For fruit trees, however, it can take up to twelve years before they bear fruit.

Earlier I mentioned growing your money, and you may be asking yourself the question, "Why would I want to grow my money?"

Growing your money is important for several reasons:

1. To combat inflation: Inflation is the increase in the price of goods and services over time. If your money isn't growing at the same rate as inflation, then your purchasing power is decreasing. By growing your money, you can help combat inflation and maintain your purchasing power.

2. To achieve financial goals: Whether it's saving for a down payment on a house, funding your retirement, or starting a business, growing your money can help you reach your financial goals more quickly.

3. To build wealth: By growing your money over time, you can accumulate wealth, which can provide financial security and stability for you and your family.

4. To take advantage of compounding: Compounding is the process of earning interest or returns on your original investment, as well as on any interest or returns that are reinvested. The longer you can keep your money invested and compounding, the greater your returns will be over time.

5. To provide a cushion for unexpected expenses: Life is full of surprises, and having a cushion of savings can help you with unexpected expenses, such as a medical emergency or job loss.

Overall, growing your money is important for achieving financial security and stability, reaching your financial goals, building wealth, taking advantage of compounding, and providing a cushion for unexpected expenses.

Before investing, it is important to do your research on the investment. Ask people about their experience doing similar investments. Seek the advice of a financial professional before making any investment decisions. Get some history about the person offering the investment opportunity. Be risk-tolerant, and don't invest more than you can lose. Diversify your portfolio by not investing all your money in a single investment opportunity. Spread your investment around so your risk is not limited to one type of asset.

The wise man saves for the future, but the foolish man spends whatever he gets. (Proverbs 21:20 – TLB).

CHAPTER 10

BE FRUGAL

I remember seeing a photo of two gentlemen standing side by side, and the question that was asked was, "Who do you think the rich person is?" The gentleman on the left had on a designer fleece jacket with a tag showing two thousand five hundred dollars (US$2,500), outdoor boot tagged four hundred dollars (US$400), wristwatch tagged sixty-five dollars (US$65), cargo pants tagged two thousand five hundred dollars (US$2,500), cell phone tagged six hundred dollars (US$600), baseball cap tagged two hundred and seventy dollars (US$270) and sunglasses tagged one thousand two hundred dollars (US$1,200), giving a total of seven thousand five hundred and thirty-five dollars (US$7,535).

The gentleman on the right wore a long sleeve oxford dress shirt tagged thirty-five dollars (US$35), dress pants tagged seventy dollars (US$70), and casual shoes tagged seventy dollars (US$70), giving a total of one hundred and seventy-five dollars (US$175).

By now you would have realized that there was some trick in this question and deduced that the rich person was the gentleman on the right with a total clothing value of One hundred and seventy-five dollars (US$175), and the poor person was the gentleman on the left with a total clothing value of seven thousand five hundred and thirty-five dollars (US$7,535). What was further revealed is that the person on the right, the rich person, had a total net worth of one billion dollars, and the one on the right, the poor person, was broke. As simple as this seems, this is a direct reflection of our society; people getting poor by trying to look rich.

If you think you need to make extravagant purchases to appear rich, you are wrong. The truly wealthy don't throw their money around. They are mindful managers.

The mindset change surrounding how you attire yourself is that you need to always be frugal rather than seeking to adorn yourself in the most expensive clothing brands. A frugal person is careful about spending money or using things when they do not need it. You may be tempted to think that being frugal is the same as being cheap, but let's clarify. A frugal person will buy quality items but will wait for a sale on genuine brand-name items so they can get it for less. However, the cheap person will just buy whatever they can get at the lowest possible price. Frugal is good, while cheap is bad.

The frugal person wears clean clothes, freshly pressed, with no threads, rips, stains, or fade. Black, white, and navy are always elegant colors that can make you look more expensive.

When it comes to doing business, the frugal person doesn't wish for more time but wishes to add more value with the same allocated time. The frugal persons don't wish for more opportunities but wish for wisdom to maximize their current opportunities. Jim Rohn, the renowned American entrepreneur, author, and motivational speaker, said it like this, "Learn how to be happy with what you have, while you pursue all that you want."

A wise person would not want to give up more of their time to work at the expense of reducing the time spent with family and friends. They instead want to add value to their existing time.

By focusing on adding value to the time you have, you can be more productive and make better use of your resources. It is important to prioritize your time and identify the most important tasks. Then, you can put your energy into completing those tasks to the best of your ability.

Another aspect of being frugal is prioritizing spending on things that truly matter to you, whether that is education or experiences with loved ones. Creating and sticking to a budget can help you track your spending, avoid overspending, and reach your financial goals.

CHAPTER 11

BE PHYSICALLY FIT

B eing physically fit is incredibly important for overall health and well-being. It makes no sense to always talk and learn about money and how to get rich but never talk about health and how to live long enough to enjoy the wealth you create.

Here are some of the reasons why you should be physically fit:

1. Reduces the risk of chronic diseases: Regular exercise and physical activity can help lower the risk of chronic diseases such as heart disease, type 2 diabetes, and certain types of cancer.

2. Improves mental health: Exercise can help reduce symptoms of depression and anxiety, improve mood, and increase self-esteem.

3. Increases energy levels: Regular exercise can improve endurance and strength, leading to increased energy levels.

4. Improves sleep: Physical activity and exercise can help improve the quality of sleep and reduce the risk of sleep disorders.

5. Helps with weight management: Regular exercise can help reduce body fat and maintain a healthy weight.

6. Strengthens bones and muscles: Exercise can improve bone density and muscle strength, reducing the risk of osteoporosis and injury.

Overall, being physically fit can lead to a healthier and happier life.

No matter how much money you have, money is not the most important thing you think about when you are feeling sick. If someone was to ask you, "Which would you choose: waking up with no money in the bank or waking up with some critical illness that had no cure?", what would be your answer? Everyone would say they would prefer to wake up with no money in the bank. This showed that health is more important than money. The fact that you have health means you can make money. In the same way, having more money will not make you physically fit. Yes, having more money can allow you to buy better food and spend more time in the gym.

Physical fitness requires consistent exercise and healthy eating habits, which may not necessarily require a lot of money. In fact, there are many affordable and even free ways to stay active and maintain a healthy lifestyle, such as walking, running, cycling, or doing bodyweight exercises at home. It is important to prioritize physical fitness as part of a healthy lifestyle, regardless of financial status.

Money is still necessary for accessing healthcare and other necessary resources. Without money, it can be difficult to pay for medical bills, medication, and other expenses related to illness. It is important to prioritize your health and seek medical attention when needed, but it is also important to have financial stability to support yourself during times of illness.

CHAPTER 12

POWERFUL SELF IMAGE

L ook the part. Dress the part. Live the part.

Some people even say, "Fake the part." Or even more pointed, "Fake it till you make it." Either way you look at it, we all need to have a positive image of ourselves, where we want to be, and start to look like that destination.

We all have an image of ourselves, and this is how we see ourselves. How you see yourself is based on the information you have, and everything you do depends on the image you see of yourself.

Some people will starve themselves to death because each time they look in the mirror, something inside them tells them they are fat, so they decide not to eat in an effort to lose weight so they can be slim. Never mind that the reality outside of them that is seen by everyone else is someone who is very much not fat, but, in their mind, they are convinced that they are fat and it would be futile for you to tell them otherwise. This is self-image: How you see yourself based on the information you have of yourself inside your mind.

In the same way, someone whose self-image tells them that they are poor, and no matter what they do, they will always be poor because their parents were poor and their grandparents were poor so it's destiny that they too will be poor. Never mind that the opportunities they have available to them can change that cycle of poverty. What they need is a paradigm shift or a renewed mind, as some would say, or they just need to reprogram their mind.

And be not conformed to this world: but be ye transformed by the renewing of your mind, that ye may prove what is that good, and acceptable, and perfect, will of God. (Romans 12:2 – KJV).

If you are going to change, then you have to look inside yourself and change what is contained there about you. You have to build an image in your mind of what you want to do and just do it. If that image is rich, then you can be rich. If that image is abundance, then you will live in abundance.

When someone has an improved self-image, they tend to view themselves in a more positive light and see their worth, abilities, and potential. This positive self-perception can translate into an abundance mindset where they believe that abundant opportunities, resources, and possibilities are available to them. They are more likely to take risks and pursue their goals because they believe in themselves and their ability to handle challenges and setbacks. This can lead to greater confidence, resilience, and success in both personal and professional endeavors.

"We Become What We Think About Most Of The Time."
—Earl Nightingale!

There are several ways to raise your self-image to another level:

1. Practice self-care: Take care of your physical and mental health. Exercise regularly, eat a healthy diet, get enough sleep, and make time for activities that bring you joy and relaxation.

2. Focus on your strengths: Identify your strengths and focus on them. You can make a list of your strengths and highlight them. Focus on developing them further.

3. Set realistic goals: Set goals for yourself that are achievable and realistic. When you achieve these goals, it will boost your confidence and self-image.

4. Surround yourself with positive people: Surround yourself with people who lift you up instead of bringing you down. Spend time with people who encourage and support you.

5. Learn to accept compliments: Accept compliments graciously and learn to internalize them. When

someone compliments you, say thank you and believe it.

6. Challenge negative self-talk: Challenge negative self-talk and replace it with positive self-talk. Be kind and compassionate to yourself.

7. Practice gratitude: Focus on what you are grateful for in your life. Gratitude can help shift your focus from negative to positive, and increase your overall sense of well-being.

Remember, building a self-image is a journey, so be patient and kind to yourself along the way.

An excellent book that will broaden your understanding of self-image is one written by Maxwell Maltz. Maxwell Maltz was an American cosmetic surgeon and author of Psycho-Cybernetics, which is a system of ideas that he claimed could improve one's self-image leading to a more successful and fulfilling life.

List the areas of your self-image that you need to
reprogram:

_____

_____

_____

_____

_____

_____

_____

_____

_____

_____

_____

_____

_____

_____

_____

_____

_____

_____

_____

_____

List the ways you will employ to reprogram and raise to another level the self-images you listed above:

_____

_____

_____

_____

_____

_____

_____

_____

_____

_____

_____

_____

_____

_____

_____

_____

_____

CHAPTER 13

BE MINDFUL OF YOUR EMOTIONS

Money, like many other things in life, can elicit strong emotions. Be mindful of your feelings surrounding money, as this can lead to unwarranted stress and, in the long term, can create diseases such as cancer. This is a documented fact in many medical journals.

One of the biggest myths concerning money is that working harder will make you richer. This is so far from the truth. The truth is, it is all about working smarter. Time is fixed, and we must be strategic to use this limited time to maximize earnings and receive success. At times, we have a fixation on the final destination as we work towards success and this causes us to lose reality with our present and not take time to enjoy each day as they come. Earl Nightingale, in his audio program, *Lead the Field*, defines success as the progressive realization of a worthy goal. He goes on to say that this means anyone who is on a course toward the fulfillment of a goal is successful, and that success doesn't lie in the achievement of a goal but it lies in the journey toward the goal.

We are successful as long as we are working towards a goal!

This definition of success may seem unpopular as it is not what the worldview on success looks like. The worldview of success means the achievement of a desired vision or planned goal. It is not the process as indicated by Earl Nightingale, but it is the destination. Another definition of success, according to the worldview, is the achievement of certain social status marked by prosperity, wealth, and fame. One way of mastering your emotions is to enjoy every step towards success and treat it as a milestone. Appreciate the progress you have made, and recognize how far you have come.

Another area where we fall down with our emotions is by accepting a victim-mentality and choosing something that is comfortable rather than that which is good for you. This is also related to a negative self-image.

An aspect of the victim-mentality when it comes to your money is when you say "I don't have the money right now to invest" or "I don't have the money to do this or to do that." The comfortable way is to say "I can't afford it," while eliminating the ways you can afford it. In this particular case, a simple way to find money to invest is to identify things you can do without and stop spending on them. The money you save can then be used to invest.

Another simple way is working a second job. You should, however, realize that a second job should be a temporary measure to achieve your particular goal, such as paying off a bill or getting money to invest. Once your goal is reached, you are done. You can then invest this money so it can earn for you. You, therefore, end up with both your job and the profits from your investments to provide earnings. For your first and second job, you are the one who is doing the work. However, when you invest your money, the money is the one that is working for you.

I am not suggesting that you starve yourself as you limit your spending, but some things are not a necessity and can be sacrificed for today so you can play tomorrow. Walking through your home collecting the items you have never used and having a garage sale with these items is another good opportunity to earn money to invest.

Mastering emotions can be a challenging task, but with consistent effort and practice, it can be achieved. Here are some tips that may be helpful:

1. Awareness: The first step to mastering your emotions is becoming aware of them. Pay attention to how you feel in certain situations and identify your triggers. This will enable you to understand your emotions better and take control of them.

2. Acceptance: Accept that emotions are a natural and normal part of life. Don't try to suppress or deny them; instead, learn to embrace them and use them as a tool to guide your decisions.

3. Perspective: Try to see things from a different perspective. When emotions are running high, it is easy to get caught up in the moment and lose sight of the bigger picture. Take a step back and evaluate things objectively.

4. Self-reflection: Take time to reflect on your emotions and how they affect your behavior. Journaling or meditating can be helpful in this process.

5. Coping mechanisms: Develop healthy coping mechanisms to deal with difficult emotions. Exercise, meditation, deep breathing or talking to a trusted friend can be effective ways to manage your feelings.

6. Emotional regulation: Practice emotional regulation techniques such as mindfulness, cognitive restructuring or assertiveness training to help you regulate your emotions in a healthy way.

Don't be controlled by your emotions!

CHAPTER 14

MULTIPLE SOURCES OF INCOME

One of the main reasons why having multiple sources of income is important is that it can provide financial security and stability. Relying on a single source of income can make you vulnerable to unexpected events such as job loss or economic downturns, leaving you in a vulnerable financial situation. Having additional sources of income can provide a safety net in such situations and give you a greater sense of financial security.

Relying on a single source of income can make you vulnerable!

Another benefit of having multiple sources of income is that it can provide greater flexibility and freedom in your lifestyle. By diversifying your income streams, you may be able to take on work that is more fulfilling or enjoyable without worrying about the financial implications. This can lead to a better work-life balance and greater overall satisfaction.

In addition, having multiple sources of income can also provide opportunities for growth and learning. By taking on different types of work or exploring new income streams, you can develop new skills and expertise that may benefit you in the long term.

Overall, having multiple sources of income can provide a range of benefits, including greater financial security, flexibility, and opportunities for growth and learning.

Invest in seven ventures, yes, in eight; you do not know what disaster may come upon the land. (Ecclesiastes 11:2 – NIV).

CHAPTER 15

DO SOMETHING

S top ticking boxes. Stop looking for loopholes. Stop being WOKE. Stop focusing on diversity and inclusion as a means to get selected. Do something! Inaction will never produce an action. People must learn to act and act for themselves for their success and the well-being of their families.

If you don't try, you will never change!

If you want to change your life, you have to make a decision to change your life and take action. Sitting around waiting for some special time that seems divinely appointed to get yourself ready for that change will not make it happen. Procrastination is a very common issue that can affect our productivity and success. The phrase "procrastination is the thief of time" means that when we procrastinate, we waste time that could be used for completing important tasks or achieving our goals. It is important to use our time wisely and avoid procrastination to ensure that we make the most of our lives.

Change requires effort and action, and without trying, people cannot expect to see positive change in their lives. It is important to note that change is a process that takes time, effort, and patience.

You must identify what changes need to be made and develop a plan of action to achieve those goals. This may involve seeking support from family, friends, or professionals, as well as developing good habits to maintain those changes.

It is also important to recognize that some changes may not happen overnight, and setbacks may occur along the way. This is why it is important to maintain a positive attitude, remain motivated, and stay focused on the end goal. Approach it with a realistic mindset and develop a well-planned strategy to achieve the desired outcomes.

Most people just don't like to take action. They seem to have this sense of fear that they will fail and, thus, they never take action. They never know what they have growing inside them, just waiting to be birthed. They could have a successful business. They could have the formula to solve world hunger, but they will never know because they never take the first step. They will never know what they could achieve. Not only will they never take the first step, but they are always telling themselves that they will start taking action tomorrow, and this tomorrow never comes.

Some of us will not move unless we can see clearly what will happen at each step three days in advance. It is like walking in the dark armed with a small kerosene lamp and trying to see beyond the next few steps of the illumination of its light hoping to see your final destination which is a mile away. But, of course, that is not possible as no one can see into the future. The crystal ball effect simply does not work. People need to get up and patiently move in the direction outlined in their plans—the direction they hope to find success.

The very definition of the word "risk" implies uncertainty and unexpected outcomes for whatever you are planning on doing. If you never take that risk, then you will never know what awaits you in the future. Imagine if you take the risk and receive a successful result. This will embolden you that there was nothing to fear. Even if you do not receive success, the fact that you had previous success will arm you to rest easy that success will come.

Success breeds confidence and discipline. One of the most important motivations for success is progress, and the fact that you have done it in the past motivates you to do it again. This also increases your capacity to make money. The experience and exposure you now have increased your mindset to a different level of expectation.

The saying "Everything worthwhile is uphill," attributed to John Maxwell, is quite applicable in this situation. John Maxwell is a number one New York Times bestselling author, coach, and speaker. Maxwell was identified as the most popular leadership expert in the world. According to Maxwell, almost everything that has value and almost everything that has purpose requires work on our part to attain it. We must put in the effort to get to where we want to go. You have to be intentional; nobody ever went up a hill by accident.

Take the risk for yourself!

Another situation that can paralyze us to a state of inaction is not wanting to change anything when we are seeing success in our present stage of life. Some people will also never realize when it is time to change, for example, when it is time to change their job to one that has better opportunities for learning and growth when they have maxed out the growth possibilities of where they are now or when it is time to start a business venture of their own.

Changes can be very scary but, again, if you do something today, something will change revealing the endless possibilities that await you.

Some of us are waiting for everything to be okay before we start enjoying life, and this too can paralyze us. You cannot wait until everything is okay to start enjoying your life. Life is unpredictable and constantly changing, and waiting for everything to be perfect will only lead to missed opportunities and regrets.

It is important to recognize that there will always be challenges and setbacks, but that doesn't mean you can't find moments of happiness and joy in between. Embracing the present moment and finding gratitude for the good in your life, no matter how small, can help bring a sense of fulfillment and positivity.

It is also important to remember that happiness is a journey, not a destination. You don't need to have everything figured out or be in a perfect situation to start enjoying your life. By focusing on building meaningful connections and engaging in activities that bring you joy, you can start experiencing the beauty of life right now.

What are the actions you need to take today?

CHAPTER 16

FROM BROKE TO AN ABUNDANCE MINDSET

People who grew up in the 1970s, and particularly those who had interactions with their grandparents, can recall the humbled life they lived. By today's standards, our grandparents seemed to have had very menial jobs. My grandparents worked as caregivers, homemakers, market vendors, and cane cutters, but it was amazing how they seemed settled in themselves and their surroundings, how they were able to make ends meet and live a comfortable life. They managed the little money they had, enough so that they were able to provide the opportunity for schooling and proper education for their children. I call those days the good old days when things and life seemed less complicated. People from the Caribbean and those of other tropical countries can remember vividly the kitchen garden just beside the kitchen steps tended by our grandmothers that seemed to provide an endless supply of food for the kitchen. Because of this, there never seemed to be a time of lack when they entered the kitchen.

In many ways, our grandparents' abundance fostered innovation, collaboration, and sharing of resources, leading to greater sustainability and resilience in the face of challenges and change.

Our grandparents' perspective of abundance was never about money and wealth, yet they seemed confident in all situations and had a strength grounded in their faith that God will supply, and He always came through for them.

But my God shall supply all your need according to his riches in glory by Christ Jesus. (Philippians 4:19 – KJV).

What examples can you pull from your grandparents' life that you can apply to your life?

Transitioning from a broke mindset to an abundance mindset can be challenging, but it is possible with the right attitude, tools, and strategies.

Here are some steps one can take to cultivate an abundance mindset:

1. Focus on gratitude: Practicing gratitude is an essential step towards an abundance mindset. Take time each day to reflect on the things you are grateful for, no matter how small, and acknowledge them. This helps to shift your focus from lack to abundance.

2. Visualize your goals: Spend time each day imagining yourself living the life you desire and focus on the positive feelings that come with it.

3. Challenge limiting beliefs: Identify any limiting beliefs you may have about money or abundance and challenge them. Adopt beliefs that align with your desired abundance.

4. Act from an abundance mindset: Make decisions from a place of abundance and avoid making choices based on fear or scarcity. Take actions that align with your goals and values, and trust that God will provide what you need to achieve them.

5. Surround yourself with abundance: Surround yourself with positive, like-minded people who embody abundance. Negative people will give you negative advice that will result in negative results. You cannot plant a mango tree and expect to reap pineapples from it.

Remember that it takes time and practice to fully embrace an abundance mindset, but with consistency and perseverance, it is possible to create a life of abundance and prosperity.

What Is A Mindset?

Your mindset is a set of beliefs that shape how you make sense of the world and yourself. It influences how you think, feel, and behave in any given situation. It means that what you believe about yourself impacts your success or failure.[5]

---

[5] What Is a Mindset and Why It Matters, By Kendra Cherry, September 20, 2022

What examples can you pull from your grandparent's life that you can apply to your life to develop the abundance mindset they lived?

_____

_____

_____

_____

_____

_____

_____

_____

_____

_____

_____

_____

_____

_____

_____

_____

_____

_____

_____

What are the things you need to let go of from your life to develop the abundance mindset your grandparents lived?

_____

_____

_____

_____

_____

_____

_____

_____

_____

_____

_____

_____

_____

_____

_____

_____

_____

_____

CHAPTER 17

OTHERS HAVING MONEY DOES NOT MEAN YOU HAVE LESS

Many grow up with the idea that the proverbial success pie is limited, particularly when they see the outward signs of what appears to be the upward mobility and positive outcome of others. We sometimes celebrate with them, but in our quiet alone times, it is hard not to feel diminished as it seems that others have outperformed us.

At this point, they typically suffer from a mentality of financial scarcity and are caught up with the fact of always looking over the fence on how the Jones are living their lives.

There is no ceiling or limit to how much money one can have. The success of others does not threaten yours or mine. It is said that much of the wealth you see is fake as you would be surprised if you get a peek into the person's wallet and bank account to see that it does not match the lifestyle being portrayed. Also, on the flip side, people who live a humble life bank account show that they can afford to live much more lavishly than they portray.

We all must be careful we do not fall into the trap where a person's success threatens us. This could drive us to the point of resentment and just pure bad mind of the success of others. This can paralyze us mentally and physically to the point where we fail to act in securing wealth and opportunities for ourselves and those we love.

It is important to focus on our own financial goals and work towards achieving them, rather than comparing ourselves to others. Building wealth takes time and effort, and staying motivated and disciplined in our financial decisions is important. It is also important to remember that wealth can be created and shared, and there are many opportunities to build it along the way. By staying focused on our financial goals and helping others when possible, we can all work towards a more prosperous future.

Celebrate with others in their success!

God can do anything, you know—far more than you could ever imagine or guess or request in your wildest dreams! He does it not by pushing us around but by working within us. (Ephesians 3:20-21 – MSG).

CHAPTER 18

BROKE AND A SLAVE TO THE SYSTEM

Money is the single most powerful tool we have to navigate this complicated world. English statesman Francis Bacon once wrote, "Money is a great servant but a bad master." Either we can control money…or it can control us." I would also choose to add to that quote from Francis Bacon the following: "Whoever controls money will also control those who are without money and that is if you find yourself on the wrong side of money and are broke."

Here are some ways that we can let money decide whether we should strive:

Money is your master if:

- You let money decide whether you should strive for something.
- You let money decide which job you should take.

- You refrain from doing things you love because of the cost.
- You refrain from getting an education because of the cost.
- You look at the price before you look at the item.
- You avoid discussing financial issues with people in your life.
- You often come into conflict about money with people in your life.
- You run out of money at the end of the month.
- You habitually spend more money than you earn.
- You hide behind the door when charities ask for donations.
- You worry about money.
- Your investments (or lack thereof) can keep you awake at night.[6]

Understanding money is critical. If you choose to master it, then money becomes a wonderful servant to you. If not, then you may not be able to control your destiny, and you could become servitude/slave to the financial system.

Money is your servant (and you are its master) if:

- You understand how much power you have to create your life, including your income and wealth.

---

[6] Is Money Your Servant or Your Master? by Beile Grünbaum | Nov 21, 2021

- You get money to work for you and not the other way around.
- You spend money to support your personal growth and development.
- You let money flow because you understand that what you send out comes back.
- You have a feeling that you'll have enough to create the life you want.
- You have not chosen a job or career based on how much you can earn.
- You spend time thinking about what you want to create in the next phase of your life.
- You understand that you can spend money to help you get to the next level.[7]

Being broke can certainly introduce financial struggles, limit one's options and freedom, and make it more difficult to achieve certain goals.

While financial resources can be a significant factor in shaping one's path in life, many people who face financial challenges find ways to overcome them and improve their situation.

Make money your servant!

---

[7] Is Money Your Servant or Your Master? by Beile Grünbaum | Nov 21, 2021

There are many other factors that can also influence a person's trajectory, such as talent, education, relationships, health, and personal drive. It is important to acknowledge the challenges that come with financial struggles and recognize the potential for growth and agency in the face of adversity.

List from above the ways you will make money your servant.

_____

_____

_____

_____

_____

_____

_____

_____

_____

_____

_____

_____

_____

_____

_____

_____

_____

_____

_____

_____

CHAPTER 19

STOP COMPARING YOURSELF TO OTHERS

We are human beings, and failure is a characteristic of all humans. We can get broke, and we should not be too hard on ourselves. It is easy to fall to the point of thinking that others are better than you. Comparing ourselves to others is also thought to be naturally embedded in our human nature. We tend to desire what other people have, but this can be detrimental to one's mental well-being.

When we compare ourselves to others, we often see the bountiful gains in people's lives and not the reality of the struggles they face. We focus on what we lack rather than our strengths and achievements. This can lead to feelings of inadequacy, low self-esteem, and even depression.

It is important to remember that everyone has their own unique path in life, and comparing ourselves to others is not a fair or accurate comparison. Instead, we should focus on our goals, progress, and growth and celebrate our accomplishments.

Some of the most successful celebrities of our time have been known to struggle with insecurities and loneliness. Sadly, they often turn to illicit drugs to find relief, but this relief is only temporary, and they soon return to a life of horror.

... for He makes His sun rise on those who are evil and on those who are good, and makes the rain fall on the righteous [those who are morally upright] and the unrighteous [the unrepentant, those who oppose Him]. (Matthew 5:45 – AMP).

The sun rises and the rain falls on all of us bar none—both the good and the not-so-good. I would also like to add on both the rich and the poor. The fact is, we all endure hard times. The failings of others are never something to rejoice about, but the observations of success that you often gravitate to are only on the surface while the truth is hidden out of sight.

One helpful tip to help us to stop comparing ourselves to others is to practice gratitude and focus on what we have rather than what we lack. Focus on the steps the other person had to take to achieve their goals and extract from them the things you can learn that you can implement in your life. This can help shift our perspective and cultivate a more positive outlook on life.

Make a careful exploration of who you are and the work you have been given, and then sink yourself into that. Don't be impressed with yourself. Don't compare yourself with others. Each of you must take responsibility for doing the creative best you can with your own life. (Galatians 6:4-5 – MSG).

Let me introduce a little spin to comparing yourself with others, and this I am calling "A Key Alternative." I spoke about learning from successful entrepreneurs and investment advisors in the chapter "Why We Don't Learn About Money in School." Imagine if instead of comparing yourself with others, you develop a strategy that says, "What would the successful entrepreneurs do?" "What would the successful investment advisors do?" Now you have turned every difficult situation into an opportunity to learn and develop, and that is an alternative that offers the key to success with a strong motivation rather than courting self-doubt.

As soon as you are settled on "the what," the next question you will naturally move to is "the how." How can you do it? How can you be a success? Then take action.

Learn and develop from the Key Alternatives!

List five situations where you compared yourself to others, then apply "The Why" and "The How" to each situation:

_____

_____

_____

_____

_____

_____

_____

_____

_____

_____

_____

_____

_____

_____

_____

_____

_____

_____

_____

_____

CHAPTER 20

IT'S NEVER TOO LATE TO LEARN

E very day brings new experiences and challenges, and there is always something new to learn. The fact that you wake up each morning presents a brand new opportunity, and the possibilities are endless. Move away from the self-defeating act of losing hope that leads you to become stagnant.

The article by Ellen Kocher titled "5 Reasons Why 50-Something Entrepreneurs Are More Successful" proposes that a 50-year-old entrepreneur is almost twice as likely to start an extremely successful company than a 30-year-old. Most of us would think that at fifty, you have reached your peak and now you are steering into retirement, but this is not the reality. The saying "age is just a number" is certainly applicable at this point.

Warren Buffet, considered to be the most successful investor of the 20th century, is still investing in his 80s. He has a net worth of 114.6 billion USD and spends most of his day reading to keep his mind sharp. The majority of his wealth came after his 50th birthday.

It's never too late to learn!

Learning is a lifelong process, and it is never too late to start. Whether you are looking to develop a new skill, deepen your knowledge on a particular subject or explore a new hobby, there are endless opportunities for learning and growth.

There are many benefits to continuing to learn throughout your life. It can help keep your mind sharp and engaged, open up new career opportunities, improve your social life, and enhance your personal development.

So, whether you are interested in taking a class, reading a book or trying out a new activity, don't hesitate to pursue your interests and continue to learn.

Embrace each day with an open mind and a desire to learn, and you will be surprised at how much you can accomplish.

We are afflicted in every way, but not crushed; perplexed, but not driven to despair… (2 Corinthians 4:8 – ESV).

Survival instincts are a fundamental driving force for humanity. From our earliest days, humans needed to find food, water, and shelter to stay alive, and these basic needs have shaped the way we live, work, and interact with the world around us so much that we have developed the ability to quickly adjust our strategic fundamental methods and learn new skills that will allow us to overcome odds and remain victorious.

Learning new skills is a part of survival!

Throughout history, humans have developed countless strategies for survival, from hunting and gathering in small tribes to building elaborate systems of agriculture, trade, and commerce. Today, we continue to rely on our instincts to ensure our safety and well-being, including stockpiling food and supplies in preparation for a natural disaster.

Of course, survival instincts don't just impact our individual lives, they also play a major role in shaping the way societies and cultures evolve. For example, our instincts to protect ourselves and our loved ones have likely contributed to the development of social norms. Similarly, our drive to accumulate resources and status may have led to the creation of economic systems and hierarchies that have fuelled both innovation and quality of life.

As long as you are ready and willing to survive and learn, then it is never too late to grow your knowledge in financial literacy. This is the knowledge you will need to arm yourself with to move from poverty to abundance.

Learning is a life-long process!

If you want to have abundance, you must have the skills of abundance, and you have to be willing to learn them. **Improve yourself every day!**

List three things that, if you learn today, will bring you more opportunities and possibilities:

_____

_____

_____

_____

_____

_____

_____

_____

_____

_____

_____

_____

_____

_____

_____

_____

_____

_____

_____

_____

CHAPTER 21

GETTING RICH AND STAYING RICH

We all spend much of our focus on building wealth and getting rich. However, we totally ignore the "What then" after we have attained wealth. Equally important as us learning the principles of building wealth is learning the principles to ensure that we remain in the position of wealth. If we don't make this a priority as well, then we risk the possibility of losing the wealth we earned and drifting back into poverty.

Getting rich and staying rich requires a combination of good financial habits and smart decision-making.

Here are some tips to help you achieve this goal:

1. Live below your means: Spend less than you earn, and always look for ways to save money. This means avoiding unnecessary expenses and setting a budget for your lifestyle.

2. Invest wisely: Invest your money in assets that appreciate over time, such as stocks, bonds, and real estate. Don't put all your eggs in one basket; always diversify your portfolio.

3. Plan for the long-term: Have a clear financial plan that includes long-term goals such as retirement, education, and buying a home. Make sure you have a solid plan in place and stick to it.

4. Stay debt-free: Avoid high-interest debts, such as credit cards, and pay off any outstanding balances as quickly as possible. Consider consolidating your debt into a single low-interest loan.

5. Stay disciplined: Consistently evaluate your investment returns and adjust your strategy as necessary. Also, stay disciplined in your spending habits, and avoid impulsive purchases.

By following these tips, you can increase your chances of getting rich and staying rich over the long term. It takes patience, discipline, and hard work to achieve financial freedom.

If people can't see what God is doing, they stumble all over themselves; But when they attend to what he reveals, they are most blessed. (Proverbs 29:18 – MSG).

CHAPTER 22

HOW TO OVERCOME YOUR LIMITING BELIEFS

Are we all programmed?

My parents had it right and, in hindsight, I think they may have had it half-right. They encouraged us to ensure we got a solid education, but their mindset of success needed more clarity in their delivery. The idea of requiring a big bank account, a new car, and a sprawling house was the determining outward factor for success that is trumped by the persons who live off-the-grid.

Persons who live off-the-grid are called off-gridders. Off-gridders are persons going to remote communities where land is cheap and they can purchase a vast amount of acres at a fraction of the cost for a city dwelling. Most of the time they have no connection to the city water mains or the city main electricity. Off-gridders utilize a well or rainwater and harvest solar electrical systems to harness the power of the sun to supply electricity to their home. Every off-gridder automatically reduces their energy and water consumption by up to 90%. Off-gridders have the option to live from everything they plant or be able to do remote work to offset some of their expenses for remote living.

The culture of work has changed, and it is no longer a requirement for a manager to look into your eyes each day to ensure you are at work, never mind that you may not be doing any work. Just the fact of them seeing you was sufficient to conclude that staff has turned up to work and is actively engaged in work. With the new media of thought-work, people are now able to work wherever they are, no matter how remote, as long as they have suitable access to the internet. With the advent of Elon Musk's Starlink technology, everyone can now access high-speed internet anywhere and anytime. The standard of work is no longer a look in the eyes but being able to meet pre-determined deadlines, which include completion dates allotted to assigned tasks.

There is no doubt in my mind that people who live off the grid have their own set of challenges to survival. Some off-gridders have fully assimilated to the off-grid life and received a personal badge of success, while others were not so fortunate and have migrated back into the corporate world, realizing that that life was not for them. Isn't this a common thread of life wherever you decide to live? Not everyone succeeds in corporate work and, at its extreme, some persons from the corporate world have even ended up homeless, sleeping in their cars or living on the streets.

What the off-grid living model has done is open the minds of everyone to the fact that there is no longer just one standard of living. A myriad of options are now available, which includes choosing to live off the land as off-gridders, tiny home living, van living, accessory dwelling units or even returning to communal living where multiple families pool their efforts as one to satisfy the needs of each other.

Have a look at Michael Reynolds, the founder of the Earthship movement "Earthship Biotecture." Michael Reynolds is an American architect based in New Mexico who is known for the design and construction of "Earthship" passive solar houses. He is a proponent of "radical sustainable living." He has overcome the odds and is living proof that successful off-grid living is possible. Testimony of this is the many disciples who follow his development and who have also received success living off-grid.

Where we live and how we work are just two of the many ways we limit ourselves in enjoying life and living an accomplished life. Limiting beliefs are beliefs that we hold over ourselves and others that restrict our potential and hinder our progress. Ray Dalio, the American billionaire investor and hedge fund manager, says when you limit yourself, you can get stuck, and this prevents you from moving forward. These beliefs can be deeply ingrained and difficult to overcome, but it is possible to challenge and shift them.

Here are some steps you can take to overcome your limiting beliefs:

1. Identify your limiting beliefs: The first step is to become aware of the beliefs that are holding you back. Pay attention to your thoughts and identify any negative self-talk or patterns of behavior that may be caused by your limiting beliefs.

2. Challenge your beliefs: Once you have identified your limiting beliefs, challenge them by asking yourself if they are true. Is there evidence to support them? What would happen if you let go of these beliefs?

3. Reframe your beliefs: Instead of focusing on limiting beliefs, try to reframe them in a positive way. For example, if you believe you are not good enough, reframe it as "I have the potential to learn and grow."

4. Take action: Overcoming limiting beliefs requires action. Take small steps toward your goals and be persistent. Celebrate your successes along the way and learn from your mistakes.

5. Seek support: As always, don't be afraid to seek support from others. Talk to a trusted friend or family member, a therapist, or a coach who can help you address your limiting beliefs and support you as you work through them.

Remember, overcoming limiting beliefs is a journey that requires patience, persistence, and self-compassion. Keep moving forward, and don't give up on yourself.

What are the limiting beliefs that you need to overcome?

_____

_____

_____

_____

_____

_____

_____

_____

_____

_____

_____

_____

_____

_____

_____

_____

_____

_____

_____

How can you overcome your limiting beliefs?

CHAPTER 23

WHAT IS THE PURPOSE OF MY WORKING

In reality, there is only one purpose served by paid employment: getting paid. That is the only real link between work and money. The other "purposes" of paid employment are other types of rewards, certainly desirable, but not directly related to getting paid. They are all equally available in unpaid activities.[8]

Ultimately, work brings money, and money brings freedom and empowerment, allowing people to chart their own paths toward happiness and life fulfillment.

I was listening to a program some time ago and the results from a critical survey were shared. I was dumbfounded by the conclusion. I tried to find the actual survey, but I have not found it as yet. In the survey, the participants were asked, "Why do people work?" The overwhelming answer was because everyone else was doing it.

---

[8] https://myprettypennies.com, The Benefits of Working for Someone Else.

After hearing this, I did a little informal survey of my own among a small group of friends, and the reality shocked me even more. All the persons internalized for a while, and none could validate with any certainty why they worked. One of the responses that got me thinking was from a young lady who had just bought her own home. She was single and certainly had achieved something momentous in her home acquisition. After mulling over the question for a while, she burst out, "Could it be that I am working to maintain the lifestyle of work? Everything I do is to make work possible. If I buy new clothes, it is for work. If I get a car, it is so I can get to work on time. If I get my hair done, it is so I look well at work. Is it that I am using work to maintain work?" This was such an eye-opener for me. I am sure I will ponder on this for a while, and I may even pen my thoughts into a book on this someday.

Don't use work to maintain work!

There are people I have helped with some aspects of their business—such as helping them to develop new revenue streams to make money—and they have asked me many times why I have not charged them. I cynically replied that I have not charged them because they cannot afford to pay me. The fact is, there is some work that I pursue that I am not looking for a paycheck. What I am looking for instead are opportunities for myself and my business. I am looking for ways where the help I provide can spin off into a business that offers value to their business. With this, I am not confined to the limit of a paycheck, but to the limit of the opportunity I have created which, in many cases, is multiple factors of the amount that would have been contained in a paycheck.

I think the result of the survey above points to the phenomenon called "The Bandwagon Effect."

This is a phenomenon in which people start doing something because everybody else seems to be doing it. It can be caused by psychological, social, and economic factors. People may want to be a part of a group that seems likely to win, be convinced something is correct because they have heard it repeated so many times or simply be influenced by their friends or relatives.[9]

This mundane thought on why we work can also be attributed to our limiting beliefs, and action needs to be taken to break free of this limitation.

It is time to invest in things that will bring value to yourself. Develop a healthy perspective on the purposes of work and how work as a tool can create a life that aligns with our values and bring happiness and fulfillment.

---

[9] What Is the Bandwagon Effect? Why People Follow the Crowd By THE INVESTOPEDIA TEAM, Updated February 05, 2023

What is the purpose of you working?

_____

_____

_____

_____

_____

_____

_____

_____

_____

_____

_____

_____

_____

_____

_____

_____

_____

CHAPTER 24

CONNECTING WITH THE RIGHT PEOPLE

It is common practice to say, "Birds of feathers flock together." The first interpretation that comes to mind is; if you run around with a loser, you will become a loser. You will pick up bad habits from them that will set you on the wrong path. Likewise, if you stick around negative people, after a while, you will become negative. A person who does not know how to fly cannot teach you to fly. A person who does not know how to drive cannot teach you how to drive.

It is important to recognize that people who have a negative or limiting mindset may not always have the best advice or guidance for those seeking abundance. You limit yourself by the company you keep.

Select friends wisely!

The phrase that says "By their fruits, you can know them" is often used to mean that the true nature of a person or thing can be determined by observing their actions or the results of their efforts. It comes from a Bible verse in the Gospel of Matthew that reads, **"By their fruits, ye shall know them. Do men gather grapes of thorns or figs of thistles?" (ESV).**

In other words, if someone consistently behaves in a certain way or produces certain results, they can be judged based on those actions or outcomes. For example, if a company consistently produces high-quality products and provides excellent customer service, it can be said that its "fruits" are good. On the other hand, if a person or organization engages in unethical behavior and causes harm to others, their "fruits" are bad.

The story of the eagle who lived like a chicken by Basab Ghosh chronicles best how you limit yourself by those around you. In this account, the egg of an eagle fell from the eagle's nest. The egg was found by a chicken who kept the egg safely among its other eggs. When all the eggs hatched, the chicken raised the eagle to be a chicken because they were all chickens. The eagle loved his home and his family, but his soul wanted more. The eagle looked up and saw a group of powerful eagles flying together and wished he could fly like those birds. The other chickens laughed out loud and remarked that he was a chicken and chickens don't fly. The eagle kept looking up at his real family and wishing he could be just like them. Every time the eagle told someone about his dreams, they told him it couldn't happen. The eagle came to think that was true. After a while, the eagle stopped having dreams and kept living as a chicken. The eagle finally died after living a long time as a chicken.

The moral of the chicken and eagle is, when you live among chickens, it is hard to soar like an eagle. Your thoughts and behaviors are greatly influenced by the people you meet with.

It is important to seek out advice and guidance from people who have achieved a level of success and have a positive mindset towards finance. This does not mean we should ignore the struggles and failures of others, but rather seek a balance between learning from their mistakes and seeking advice from those who have achieved financial success.

Ultimately, our mindset and beliefs can greatly impact our financial success, so it is important to surround ourselves with positive and supportive people who can help us reach our goals.

A well-known and repeated proverb says, "Tell me who your friends are, and I will tell you who you are." It is an old Spanish saying that means you can predict a person's behavior by analyzing the people they hang out with.

Iron sharpeneth iron; so a man sharpeneth the countenance of his friend. (Proverbs 27:17 – KJV).

Describe the people who are around you:

_____

_____

_____

_____

_____

_____

_____

_____

_____

_____

_____

_____

_____

_____

_____

_____

_____

_____

_____

_____

What are you learning from the people around you?

_____

_____

_____

_____

_____

_____

_____

_____

_____

_____

_____

_____

_____

_____

_____

_____

_____

_____

Are the things you are learning good for you?

_____

_____

_____

_____

_____

_____

_____

_____

_____

_____

_____

_____

_____

_____

_____

_____

_____

_____

CHAPTER 25

RETHINK YOUR VIEWS OF MONEY

T alking about money can be uncomfortable for many people, but it is an important part of managing your personal finances.

Here are a few tips to help you get more comfortable discussing money:

1. Start small: Begin by talking about money with people you trust, such as your significant other, a trusted friend or family member. Start with simple topics like budgeting or saving money.

2. Practice: Like any skill, the more you practice, the easier it becomes. Take some time to learn more about personal finance by reading books, listening to podcasts or attending financial literacy courses. You will feel more confident talking about money as you become more knowledgeable.

3. Set boundaries: It is important to have clear boundaries when discussing money with others. Determine what topics are off-limits and what information you are comfortable sharing. Communicate these boundaries clearly to others and respect their boundaries as well.

4. Stay positive: Talking about money doesn't have to be negative or stressful. Instead, approach the conversation with a positive attitude. Highlight your achievements and successes and be open to learning from others.

Remember, talking about money is essential for managing your finances. By practicing these tips, you will become more comfortable discussing money and taking control of your financial future.

"...money answereth all things." (Ecclesiastes10:19 - KJV).

CHAPTER 26

FAILURE IS A PART OF SUCCESS

"If you don't try at anything, you can't fail...it takes backbone to lead the life you want." —Richard Yates

When we strive for success, we are bound to face failures, and it is through these failures that we learn valuable lessons. In fact, it is often said that failure is a wonderful teacher. Failure is often viewed as a stepping stone toward success because it allows us to learn from our mistakes and improve ourselves.

You need to realize that failure is not the end but rather an opportunity to grow, improve and gain new insight. Everyone fails at some point in their life, and it doesn't define their worth or potential. When we fail, we can learn from our mistakes, identify areas that need improvement, and come up with new strategies to achieve our goals.

Success often comes after multiple failures and setbacks!

Don't give up; keep pushing forward and embrace failure as a stepping stone toward success.

It is important to embrace failure as a part of the journey toward success. Don't let any setbacks discourage you. Keep pushing forward and learning from your failures until you achieve your goals. Remember, every successful person has been through a series of failures before reaching their goals. Everyone knows Michael Jordan, who is considered to be the greatest basketball player of all time and arguably the greatest athlete of all time. Michael Jordan often recounts the countless times he failed—times when he did not dunk that critical shot that would have changed the results of the game and made history. If he had only made that shot, the team would have won the game, but many times it did not happen. He never gave up. He stuck with it and now has the title of greatness and the financial success to go with it.

Use failure to make you stronger!

The Lord upholds all who fall and lifts up all who are bowed down. (Psalm 145:14 – NIV).

More than that, we rejoice in our sufferings, knowing that suffering produces endurance, and endurance produces character, and character produces hope, and hope does not put us to shame, because God's love has been poured into our hearts through the Holy Spirit who has been given to us. (Romans 5:3-5 – ESV).

An abundant mindset does not fall prey to failure but sees it for what it is; an opportunity for future greatness. You can't be happy unless you learn to be satisfied with what you have now. Let go of the need for instant gratification and practice gratitude for the now.

"Failure is not the opposite of success, it's part of success."
—Arianna Huffington

List five failures in your life that you know, without a doubt, made you stronger:

_____

_____

_____

_____

_____

_____

_____

_____

_____

_____

_____

_____

_____

_____

_____

_____

_____

_____

_____

_____

CHAPTER 27

FAITH: ALL THINGS ARE POSSIBLE

Faith, in a religious or spiritual context, can give individuals a sense of hope and belief in something greater than themselves. This can foster a positive mindset and lead to a greater sense of abundance in one's life. Faith can also encourage individuals to be grateful for what they have in their life, rather than focusing on what they lack. This can create a positive perspective and cultivate an abundance mindset.

Some individuals may view their faith as a source of guidance, motivation, and inspiration, and they believe, without a shadow of a doubt, that this can help them make decisions and take actions that align with their goals and values, which can ultimately lead to a greater sense of abundance in their lives.

It is worth noting that an abundance mindset can also be developed through various other practices, such as gratitude exercises, positive self-talk, and focusing on one's strengths. If that is what you believe, then that is what you believe.

An abundance mindset is all about believing that there are endless possibilities and opportunities available to you, rather than dwelling on scarcity and limitations. When you have an abundance mindset, you tend to focus on a positive outlook and be open to new experiences.

This type of mindset hinged on your faith helps you overcome challenges and take risks that might have otherwise seemed impossible. It can also empower you to achieve your goals by believing that success is within reach.

As stated in earlier chapters, an abundance mindset isn't just about material wealth. It is also about cultivating a mindset that allows you to find joy in life's simple things and be grateful for what you have and the stage you are at in life. With an abundance mindset, you can approach life with a sense of optimism and enthusiasm that can lead to greater happiness and fulfillment.

Achieving mastery is not about the person next to you; it is about you and what you are comfortable with. It is about culturing the mindset of believing by faith that success is possible and that you can do it. You can even say that it is ordained for you by your faith in God.

"...all things are possible to him who believes." (Mark 9:23 – NKJV).

Some people make decisions for social acceptance rather than for gain. Their motivation is to please, through likes and shares, a faceless competitor or critic who they may never meet. To them, it is just a part of the social game, so much so, that if they were to ever meet that critic, all they would have to say is, "Who are you again?" and "How do I know you?" They are clueless about your very existence.

If you allow people to project their fear onto you, you won't live!

Why would you want to chance your very existence on such a fickle individual? God is able, and I would think you stand a better outcome by holding on to His truth that will never change.

Jesus looked at them and said, "With man this is impossible, but with God all things are possible." (Matthew 19:26 – NIV).

CHAPTER 28

FRIENDSHIP/YOUR TRIBE

I remember seeing an interview with an elderly homeless gentleman who looked to be in his 70s that reported to the interviewer that he felt alone. During the interview, tears started to flow from the man's eyes as he berated his present situation. What was striking to me was not the tears but the sadness I could see in his eyes. It is said that the eyes are the windows to the soul, and his eyes were sad. His pupils were fully dilated, and they showed an emptiness.

Feeling alone is a normal human experience. You can feel lonely when you are by yourself or even when you are in a room full of people. When you don't feel connected with anyone, or you feel like no one understands you, you might feel as though you are completely alone, even if you are around friends or family.

Friendship is a lovely relationship without which life seems dull. It is the relationship with our friends that teaches us to share, love, care and, most importantly, helps us to fight the odds and be successful. Having true friends acts as a boon.

Friends increase the sense of belongingness and generate a feel-good factor.

"One who has unreliable friends soon comes to ruin, but there is a friend who sticks closer than a brother." (Proverbs 18:24 – NIV).

Friendship isn't something to be taken lightly!

Building an abundance mindset also includes building what I call your tribe. These are the persons with whom you share the same customs, beliefs and have common character, occupation or interest. These are the persons who truly understand your vision and help you cultivate meaningful relationships that will last a lifetime. Your tribe gives you pleasant, sincere advice, and challenges you to meet your highest good.

Finding your tribe or creating it is so important to your happiness and inner peace. When you surround yourself with people who get it, it allows you to be your true self. The mask can come off, and you can stop wasting energy on being someone you are not.

The moments we share with our tribe can be some of the most meaningful and memorable experiences in our lives. In today's fast-paced world, it can be easy to get caught up in work, school or other responsibilities, but it is important to make time for the people in our lives who matter most. Make plans and spend time with your tribe and focus on being present during those moments.

Enjoy the time you spend with your friends!

Not having a like-minded community can make things for us difficult and unenjoyable, and it can take longer for us to achieve what we want.

CHAPTER 29

MASTER YOUR TIME

Managing your time effectively is essential for achieving success in most activities we do. Sometimes we may even feel like there aren't enough hours in a day to complete everything. Enhancing your time management skills can help you accomplish more in a shorter timeframe, and it all starts with building a success mindset.

The success mindset says we should be happy with the things that are working, and don't focus on those not working yet. Simply put, prioritize. Some people would say this has been pragmatic, like the glass being half full or half empty. However, it is about prioritizing tasks based on importance and urgency so you know exactly what needs to be done first. Prioritize the tasks that must be completed today, and put those that can wait until tomorrow near the bottom of your list.

First, it is important to understand that your attitude towards time is essential for managing it effectively. You must be willing to accept responsibility and take ownership of your decisions. Developing an attitude of determination and being self-motivated will help you stay focused on achieving your goals, no matter how challenging they may seem.

In addition to developing the success mindset, setting specific goals can provide structure and direction as you strive for success. Goals should be achievable and realistic, yet challenging enough to keep you motivated and working hard towards meeting them. Breaking down large tasks into smaller steps also makes them easier to manage and makes progress more visible, which can boost morale further.

You can start taking control of your time by establishing a success mindset and setting realistic goals. With the right mindset in place, it is time to move on to developing strategies for better time management.

We have all struggled with procrastination at some point or another. We struggle to make decisions as people, and actions can be put off, disregarded or avoided. Loss, insecurity or feelings of inadequacy can result from procrastination. We hold ourselves accountable for our laziness, perfectionism or failure phobia. It may result in depressive symptoms. In some extreme situations, it may result in burnout. Our mental health, self-talk, and negative emotions are all impacted by procrastination.

We never come out of procrastination in a better place. We must comprehend what is procrastination, and know how to stop doing it.

Choose wisely when and how you spend your time!

"Look carefully then how you walk, not as unwise but as wise, making the best use of the time, because the days are evil. Therefore do not be foolish, but understand what the will of the Lord is." (Ephesians 5:15-17 – ESV).

What strategies can you implement to maximize your time?

_____

_____

_____

_____

_____

_____

_____

_____

_____

_____

_____

_____

_____

_____

_____

_____

_____

_____

CHAPTER 30

WHAT IS YOUR VISION?

"In the end, people will judge you anyway, so don't live your life impressing others; live your life impressing yourself." —Eunice Camacho Infante

Your vision is your most important dream or mental picture. It can also be a set of dreams and long-term goals. A vision defines the optimal desired future state; it tells of what you would like to achieve over a longer time.

Create your own vision today of how you can transition from a Broke Mindset to an Abundance Mindset. Let me remind you of a few of the points outlined in this book that can help you do just that.

Money is not a finite resource that is divided up among individuals. Just because someone else has money, does not necessarily mean you have less. It is important to focus on creating and building your own wealth rather than comparing yourself to others. Know your purpose and walk in that purpose every day.

Having a vision helps you prioritize your life, allowing you to walk away from certain people or activities that don't serve your purpose. Your main drive should be to stay motivated, particularly when things get tough, so you can set and meet short and long-term goals.

Take small steps toward your goals and be persistent!

Success does not fall from the sky. It does not happen by chance; it takes work. You must be ready for success and ready to take action when opportunities come.

Financial success is not the only measure of a fulfilling life. Building strong relationships, pursuing hobbies and passions, and positively impacting our communities are all important aspects of a fulfilling life. While financial stability is important, it is just one piece of the puzzle. So, let's work towards our financial goals, build meaningful relationships, pursue personal passions and hobbies, and give back to our communities.

Abundance is the attitude or mindset about feeling happy with what you have. We need to separate this from you having billions in your bank account, as even people with this vast supply of money are not living a happy life.

Find a balance that works for you and your individual circumstances by focusing on your own goals and priorities. Create a life that aligns with your values and reap happiness and fulfillment.

Where there is no vision, the people perish: but he that keepeth the law, happy is he. (Proverbs 29:18 – KJV).

My people are destroyed for lack of knowledge: because thou hast rejected knowledge, I will also reject thee. (Hosea 4:6a – KJV).

If any of you lack wisdom, let him ask of God, that giveth to all men liberally, and upbraideth not; and it shall be given him. (James 1:5 – KJV).

Remember the power of family and the tribe of persons you have around you. You don't have to try to do everything for yourself. Rather than comparing yourself with others, share your vision with them and invite them to work with you and reap an abundant life.

Move from scarcity thinking to abundance thinking. Stop thinking there is not enough but believe there is always enough. Rich Wilkenson Jr. says it like this "A scarcity mindset will always keep you poor."

If you don't try, you will never change. If you are going to change, then you have to look deep inside yourself and change what is contained there about you. You have to build an image in your mind of what you want to do and just do it. If that new image is rich, then you can be rich. If that image is abundance, then you will live in abundance.

"They say money don't bring you happiness... I say neither does being broke..." —*Unknown Author*

"Money is not the most important thing in life, but it does affect everything that is important..." —*Robert Kiyosaki*

What is your vision to move from broke to an abundance mindset?

_____

_____

_____

_____

_____

_____

_____

_____

_____

_____

_____

_____

_____

_____

_____

_____

_____

_____

_____

PLEASE LEAVE A REVIEW ON AMAZON

Hello there!

If you have read this far in my book, you have learned some new skills that equipped you to move to an abundance mindset.

It has been an amazing journey to get this book completed, and I am excited to finally share it with the world.

I humbly ask that you leave an honest review on your Amazon portal for my book. Early reviews are the single most important factor in determining if a book succeeds, so I am incredibly thankful for people like you who I can rely on to leave one.

Reviews should only be 1-2 sentences and should take about 30 seconds to write (and would make a huge difference for me).

Finally, I wanted to give you a heads-up that Amazon can sometimes block or remove reviews if they deem our digital relationship too close or if your account is too new. This is few and far between, so I am sorry if you run into this, and thank you all the more for your support!

Thanks so much for your support. I deeply appreciate it.

Best,
Zeelah S. Davis